I0360687

Original title:
The Fiddle-Leaf Fig Blues

Copyright © 2025 Creative Arts Management OÜ
All rights reserved.

Author: Oliver Bennett
ISBN HARDBACK: 978-1-80581-718-5
ISBN PAPERBACK: 978-1-80581-245-6
ISBN EBOOK: 978-1-80581-718-5

Lengthening Shadows of Indoor Life

In the corner, a plant stands tall,
Leafy giant, watching all.
I water it, think I might win,
But it just droops, where to begin?

Sunbeams dance, while I sit late,
Trying to coax it into fate.
I talk to it like a long-lost friend,
It nods back, just to pretend.

Dust bunnies waltz along the floor,
As I ponder if it wants more lore.
With a light joke, I call it Joe,
I swear it chuckles, or maybe I go.

Fork in the road, it sighs with glee,
Should I be watering it, or by the TV?
Life’s a mix, of sun and shade,
Guess indoors, wildness is laid!

An Indoor Embrace

In my room, the leaves do sway,
Caught in sunlight, they dance all day.
But when I water, oh what a mess,
A little droop turns to plant distress.

My green friend loves a gentle chat,
Yet spills dirt when I clap and pat.
I swear it gives me a cheeky grin,
As if it knows it's wearing thin.

Reflections in Parched Soil

Oh soil so dry, a desert vast,
I fear I've neglected, let shadows cast.
The leaves are curling, taking their toll,
A thirsty plant with a thirsty soul.

I sprinkle drops, a guilty flood,
And consider how we've both been shrud.
Beneath the light, it surely knows,
I'm dodging blame, for how it grows.

Anthems of the Overwatered

The pot has turned into a soggy mess,
With roots so drenched, they scream distress.
My poor plant sings a dripping tune,
As I wonder if I've washed away its bloom.

Yet in this swamp, it holds its ground,
The leaves won’t give up, they're fiercely proud.
With every drop that falls like rain,
I smile at how we share this pain.

Pining for the Outdoors

Through the window, sunlit beams call,
As this green buddy starts to sprawl.
Yet bound indoors, it glances outside,
My little plant with a longing stride.

“Oh for the sun, the wind, the cheer!”
I swear it sighs, “I want to be here!”
I promise someday, we’ll frolic free,
Just you and me, fresh air with glee.

Eclipsed by Their Beauty

In the corner, it's quite a sight,
Leaves spread wide, basking in light.
I thought I'd shine, just a teeny bit,
But they outshine me, oh, what a hit!

I wore my best hat, all full of flair,
But they just grew taller, without a care.
I tried to strut, my confidence high,
Yet they just waved, oh my, oh my!

Understretching Shadows

Their shadows stretch far, like a game,
While I'm left wondering who's to blame.
I tried to dance, to sway with grace,
But those leaves laughed, they stole my space!

I tripped over roots, knocked off a shoe,
These leafy giants, oh what they do!
With every twist, I lose my groove,
I think they're plotting to make me move.

Secrets in the Potting Soil

Deep in the dirt, whispers abound,
What are the secrets that lie underground?
I scooped a handful, looked for the clues,
Found only worms, wearing shiny shoes!

The plants exchange glances, oh so sly,
What gossip they share, I can only pry.
With every sprout, there’s laughter in bloom,
My garden of jesters, my leafy room!

The Quiet Solace of Leaves

In the stillness, they sway with ease,
While I flail about, like a bee in the breeze.
“Oh calm down!” they whisper, with a rustling cheer,
“Life is a party, don’t live in fear!”

I join in the fun, try to keep cool,
But their quiet chic just makes me a fool.
So I laugh with the leaves, in this leafy affair,
Maybe one day, I’ll grow some flair!

A Tale of the Unseen Gardener

In the corner stood a plant, so tall,
Its leaves like hands, reaching for a ball.
But where's the gardener, we wonder aloud,
Hidden away, just peeking through the crowd.

Water spills like laughter, pots in a row,
Soil on the carpet, but who wants to know?
Each leaf is a riddle, every stem a joke,
A secret life lived, aside from the cloak.

The Quiet Struggle for Light

Each morning it twists, a dance for the sun,
Leaning and swaying, its battle's begun.
Yet the curtains close tight, a stubborn old foe,
Shadows are sneaky, they want all the show.

Lamp on the desk holds the spotlight so bright,
But does it matter? Not in this fight!
The plant gives a sigh, a dramatic affair,
"Who knew a green friend could need so much air?"

Whispers of Green

In whispers it shares, tales of the night,
When moonbeams waltz, giving leaves a slight fright.
“I heard them complain, those dusty old buds,
Saying more light means fewer plant thuds!”

But then came a breeze, bringing in change,
Turning those grumbles into something strange.
Dancing and prancing, they wore silly hats,
A party for greens, but where are the mats?

Echoes in the Leaves

Listen closely, you'll hear them giggle,
Leaves telling secrets, a funny little wiggle.
"I swear I just saw a spider take flight,
He was giving a speech, oh what a sight!"

With every soft rustle, a chuckle unfolds,
Even the roots, have some stories to hold.
A vine once suggested a game of charades,
But others just laughed, saying "stop with your trades!"

Glistening in Gloom

In a pot that's far too small,
A leafy giant stands so tall.
Its leaves are bright, yet slyly pout,
Wondering what this fuss is about.

Water me once, then once again,
Oh dear, did I drown the friend?
With every droop and every curl,
I find joy in this leafy swirl.

Sunshine plays hide and seek here,
It shines, then vanishes, oh dear.
My plant is confused, what shall I do?
Dance around, sing a tune or two!

So here's to plants with quirky style,
Who grow and laugh, maybe just a mile.
In their shadows, we'll gently sway,
Through leafy dances, here we'll stay.

Unraveling a Leafy Story

A tale of leaves, they start to tell,
Once perky, now they look like hell.
With fingers crossed, I check for pests,
What's the secret to their leafy quests?

Once lush and green, now slightly brown,
They seem to wear a vacant frown.
So I chat and coax with silly rhymes,
Hoping they'll thrive and beat the times.

I sprinkle love with a dash of grace,
In hopes to brighten their sad little face.
Yet here they stand, with a ghostly air,
A strange ensemble, quite beyond compare.

Each leaf a page, with tales to share,
Of sunny days and moments rare.
Together we laugh, what a funny scene,
In this leafy plot, we reign supreme.

Tender Growths in Shady Corners

In the corner where the shadows play,
A plant stands guard, in its own way.
With stems that twist and roots that bind,
It winks and whispers, 'Life's a grind!'

A sip of water, a dash of sun,
My leafy friend thinks it's all in fun.
It sways and bends, a dance on air,
"Just look at me, without a care!"

Every day's a leafy fashion show,
With styles that change, and oh, the glow!
But when it droops, I must confess,
I toss a joke, and it feels so blessed.

So here's to corners where plants reside,
Where leafy spirits and giggles collide.
In tender growths, we find our way,
Bantering back as we seize the day.

An Invitation to Journey Green

Come gather ‘round, it’s time to play,
With a leafy friend who steals the day.
In hues of green, they wave hello,
With mischief hiding in every row.

Shall we dance in the morning light?
With leaves that ripple, oh what a sight!
A nudge and giggle, together we’ll grow,
In this little patch, where fun will flow.

Every leaf a map to explore,
With secrets whispered, oh, so much more.
They beckon us to join the fun,
In this green carnival, we’ve just begun.

So take a step, with hearts in cheer,
Join the journey, the end is near.
In the land of plants, let laughter sound,
With leafy friends, new joys abound.

Stillness Among the Vining

In corners where sunlight softly plays,
A leafy giant hums through the days.
With roots deep in laughter, it sways with ease,
A nodding friend in a world of tease.

Potted in style, it takes quite the stance,
Giving advice through a leafy dance.
"Water me gently," it seems to say,
While I chuckle back – not today, no way!

Its verdant limbs reach for whispers of fun,
Stories of sunshine and leaves having fun.
In stillness, it savors the gossip around,
Of all those squirrels who play on the ground.

So here's to the plant in the slice of light,
With mischievous leaves, it knows how to bite.
Amidst all the vining and playful tricks,
The best kind of stillness keeps blending the mix.

The Pulse of Indoor Life

Amidst a sea of pots and bright hues,
A leaf on the windowpane sings the blues.
Each curl and twist holds a tale of cheer,
"Come look closer, bring laughter near!"

Chasing dust bunnies, this plant knows the score,
Dropping wise cracks from its leafy core.
Absorbing the vibes of the everyday grind,
With roots in the drama, it's one of a kind.

In the heart of the living room, it reigns,
A jester in green, shedding joy like rain.
Whispers of humor in its leafy embrace,
A quirky companion in this lively space.

With each gentle rustle, it's ready to play,
The pulse of the indoors, come join in the fray.
Unfurling its charm with each flirtatious wave,
A leafy performer, this plant is quite brave!

The Dance of Stems and Leaves

When morning breaks with a hop and a glance,
This green friend rises, ready to dance.
With stems that sway to the tune of the breeze,
Its leaves shimmy softly, oh, what a tease!

In the rhythm of sunlight, it twirls round and round,
Flashing its colors, joyously unbound.
Each leaf, like a dancer, takes part in the show,
Unfurling its edges, a remarkable flow.

Outside the window, the world rushes by,
But here in this pot, we just laugh and sigh.
A tango of chlorophyll, bright and absurd,
In this leafy ballet, not a word is heard.

So join in the fun with a jiggle and sway,
Where stems make the rules in this green cabaret.
In every small twist lies a chuckle, a groove,
The dance of the leaves is all about the move!

Hues of Quiet Reflection

In silence it beckons with colors sublime,
A leafy philosopher, taking its time.
With shades of green, and light catching tears,
It whispers softly, dissolving our fears.

Against the wall, it leans back and grins,
Observing our lives, where chaos begins.
A canvas of calm in a busy frame,
While pondering kindness and playing the game.

Fingers of sunlight caress its broad back,
Nurturing wisdom in shades of off-black.
It holds little secrets tucked deep in its bowl,
In hues of quiet, it calms the whole soul.

Can you hear it chuckling? A curious thought,
In the comfort of stillness, we find what we've sought.
With echoes of laughter, we lean in to share,
In the hues of reflection, we breathe in the air.

The Art of Indoor Serenades

In the corner, a leaf doth sway,
I hum my tune, it steals the day.
Twirl my chair, a dance of sorts,
With green companions, I hold court.

A quirk or two, a pot so wide,
They judge my moves, no place to hide.
I sing a hymn to chlorophyll,
The crowd of leaves, they get their fill.

With each off-key and silly sound,
The branches sway, they bounce around.
In indoor realms, I find my muse,
Among my plants, I'm never bruised.

So let them grow, and let me croon,
A concert held beneath the moon.
I sprout my joy, they soak it in,
Together we thrive, each and every sin.

Rooted in Solitude

Nestled deep in a ceramic home,
A stunning plant with thoughts to comb.
I sip my tea, it watches me,
Dialogues bloom, just let it be.

No chatter here, but roots that cling,
They nod and sway, as if they sing.
My friend, my green, my silent mate,
In solitude, we share our fate.

Alone, I jest with every twirl,
It fluffs its leaves, a leafy swirl.
I drop a joke, it sways right back,
Indoor life, a giddy track.

Together in this cozy place,
We plant our dreams, a leafy space.
Though silent, still the love we share,
A rooted bond, beyond compare.

Sunlight's Forgotten Melodies

Beams of gold in indoor realms,
Chasing dust like wayward elms.
The leaves and I, in bright embrace,
We wiggle to the sun's soft chase.

A lazy hum fills up the air,
Plants groove about without a care.
Mirthful vines twist in a spin,
While sunbeams dance on leafy skin.

The spotlight fades, the leaves all pout,
I shake and shimmy, twist about.
Green serenades in every glow,
Who knew that plants could steal the show?

So here we bask, with smiles wide,
No lack of light; in joy, we glide.
Together basking, leaf and soul,
In forgotten melodies, we stroll.

An Exposure of Greens

In the living room, oh what a sight,
Vibrant greens basking in the light.
They peep around with curious eyes,
As I juggle potted plants and sighs.

Dirt on my shirt, a shovel here,
As back to potting, I hold dear.
Cacti chuckle from every shelf,
But my leafy friends, they never scoff.

Every sprout a secret shade,
In photo ops, they never fade.
With each new leaf, a tale retold,
A family of greens, so brave and bold.

So let's parade our hues of bright,
In mini jungles, pure delight.
An exposure of greens, what a thrill,
In my wild garden, dreams instill.

Secrets Swaddled in Green

In a pot so deep and wide,
A leafy wonder starts to hide.
Whispers of sunlight, laughter in air,
'Why don't humans stop and stare?'

Dust bunnies dance like they own the place,
While soil plays tag in this cozy space.
Mossy hats and witty charms,
Secret gardens mean no alarms.

The squirrel's tales from dusk till dawn,
Watch as the plot thickens on the lawn.
Every leaf holds a funny twist,
A comedy script that can't be missed.

Garden gnomes humorously preen,
Braving the leaves of vibrant green.
In this world where plants partake,
Laughter grows with every shake.

A Chronicle of Chlorophyll

Once a sprout of hope confined,
With chlorophyll brewing, oh so kind.
It brushed against a flower’s tease,
‘I’m the top dog with the biggest leaves!’

Sun whispers softly, 'Grow a little,'
While roots below meet to riddle.
‘What’s it like up there, dear friend?’
‘Busy daydreams that never end!’

Chasing shadows, playing peek-a-boo,
With a breeze that tickles through.
Picky bugs come for a feast,
Turning casual chats to a leafy beast.

So come sit under this leafy crown,
Where laughter's worn like a leafy gown.
Each moment shared brings a chuckle bright,
In the green embrace of the gentle light.

Sighing with the Sapling

There's a sapling with quite the flair,
Dreaming big in the warm air.
'Why're humans so tall and grand?'
'They keep forgetting where they stand!'

Its leaves giggle with playful prance,
Mocking the squirrels in their dance.
Every breeze is a cheeky jest,
'You'll never outgrow this leafy nest!'

Once a twig, now full of sass,
Did it really grow this fast?
Pulling pranks on the garden cat,
Sticking out leaves where it's just flat.

Beneath the sun's warm, glowing beam,
A sapling chases its wild dream.
With every sigh, it makes a scene,
A little legend draped in green.

Stretched Imaginations Under Leaves

Beneath the canopy, dreams do flinch,
Every leaf's guard has a little pinch.
'What's more fun than growing tall?'
'Finding shade for a great leaf brawl!'

In a pot where thoughts expand,
A kaleidoscope of green so grand.
'How about a diving board?' they grin,
'Or maybe a trampoline to spin?'

Ticklish roots in playful tease,
Stretching imaginations with the breeze.
Leak a joke through the morning dew,
'Come join the fun, it's a leafy zoo!'

From a tiny seedling to a leafy king,
The tales of laughter are evergreen.
In laughter's warmth, together they thrive,
Stretching imaginations to feel alive.

Echoes of a Thriving Spirit

In the corner, green and grand,
Leaves waving like a hand.
But oh, my friend, don’t you see?
It's all just a leafy parody!

Dancing leaves with a twist and twirl,
Chasing sunlight with a haughty whirl.
But when the cat strolls by, it's clear,
Those playful moves turn to leafy fear!

Who knew a plant could take the stage?
Yet here I am, caught in this cage.
With each new sprout, I laugh and grin,
Just waiting for my next silly spin!

So here’s to the greens with tales to tell,
In our lively dance we do so well.
Life’s a show and I’m the muse,
With each sly joke, I shake off the blues!

The Weight of a Leafy Crown

Oh, look at me, I'm quite a sight,
A leafy crown, oh what delight!
But with every inch of leafy bliss,
Comes the weight of a daily miss.

When friends come by for a chat or two,
They nod and smile with nothing to do.
Yet behind those grins I sense despair,
Who will care for my fragile hair?

The sunlight's great, I know it's true,
But what's a queen without her crew?
Leaves shaking under the royal load,
Watch out, here comes the wind's bold road!

A crown so grand, yet so absurd,
Stand tall, I say, but now I'm stirred.
For no leaf dreams of grassy fields,
Just a throne where laughter yields!

Fragments of a Tropical Daydream

In this little pot, wonders dwell,
A tropical dream that whispers well.
I stretch and bend, elongate my form,
Hoping my roots can weather the storm.

Colorful knick-knacks rise and fall,
As I wave my leaves, a leafy call.
Daydreams shimmer like a starry haze,
While folks chuckle in a leafy maze.

Oh, how I long for a sunny glide,
Friends come to poke me and confide.
Yet all I offer is a teasing sway,
How do you like my leafy display?

Through laughter and light, we share this fate,
In quips and tales, we navigate.
The sun radiates, our joys entwine,
In this green realm, we laugh and dine!

The Lament of the Overlooked Green

In the room, I sit all forlorn,
With leaves so lush, yet I’m still scorned.
The sofa holds all the chats with glee,
While I wait here for my cup of tea.

Oh, how I wished to be in the light,
But here in the shade, I hide from the sight.
Splendid leaves, too proud to beg,
While others bask, I pose like a peg.

Friends gather 'round, they drink and cheer,
Forgotten I stand, in a lonely sphere.
But wait, oh wait, I’ve got a move!
With every leaf, I aim to groove!

I may be green, but I’ve got vibes,
In whispers shared, my spirit thrives.
So raise a glass, and share the laugh,
For this leafy king, I’m in my half!

An Unfurling of Longing

In the corner sits a friend,
With leaves like giant hands.
Stretching toward the window,
Dreaming of far-off lands.

Each morning brings a shuffle,
A dance without a care.
Whispers of ambition,
In sunlight's tender glare.

For every curl and crinkle,
There's a giggle from above.
Too wild to be tamed now,
Yet yearning for some love.

Oh, to brave the open air,
And bask in the delight.
But here they sway and wiggle,
Our greens of pure delight.

A Leaf's Quiet Resilience

A leaf that barely fluttered,
Hangs on without a care.
Through storms and sassy breezes,
It shakes its leafy hair.

With spots and sags aplenty,
It wears a fuzzy grin.
Each tear and dent a story,
Of where it's been and been.

They say that leaves are fragile,
But this one knows the way.
It spins a yarn of laughter,
As if it loves to play.

No need for fancy potting,
Or soil of royal blend.
For in the face of chaos,
Our leaf will never bend.

Tales from the Rooted

Beneath the soil lies a party,
With roots that twist and twirl.
Tangled up like gossip,
In nature's bustling world.

Each anchor holds a secret,
Of dreams and rainy days.
They giggle to each other,
In their viney, earthy ways.

With every shade and shimmer,
They boast of age and grace.
While topside life is funny,
Below’s a racing race.

So here’s to all the rooted,
May we never lose our grip.
And when we strut our green stuff,
We’ll salute with every sip.

Breaths of a Green Sanctuary

In my quirky little garden,
Where plants stand tall and proud.
Each breath a hint of mischief,
In humid, leafy shrouds.

They whisper secrets softly,
As the breeze begins to play.
These greens like jolly jesters,
Float dreams of sunny days.

A sprinkle of imagination,
Turns water into bus.
With every sip, they chuckle,
And bask in healthy fuss.

The air is fresh with laughter,
As blooms burst into song.
In this vibrant green retreat,
We know we all belong.

Notes on a Leaf's Journey

A leaf set out for a grand tour,
Dreaming of sunbeams and cheer-soaked allure.
But a gust of wind caught it by surprise,
Now it's lost in a tree with a view of the skies.

While the other leaves laugh, it begins to fret,
Thought it was clever, but now it's a pet.
Hitching a ride on a branch up so high,
Chasing clouds and wishing to fly.

With every sway, it takes in the sights,
Observing the world from dizzying heights.
Even the birds chirp a snicker or two,
"Who knew the plant could enjoy something new?"

Lost in thoughts of where it should be,
Coming to terms with its whimsical spree.
Once seedling dreams in a pot so confined,
Now free as a dancer in a place undefined.

Seasons of a Silent Companion

In spring, it sprouts in earnest delight,
Chasing the warmth, avoiding a fright.
But summer's heat gives it quite a scare,
"Too much sun and I'll soon need a chair!"

When autumn arrives, it starts shedding flair,
"What's the point? Do these garments compare?"
With a rustle and shuffle, leaves wave goodbye,
Its fashion sense flounders; oh, how time flies!

As winter descends, it huddles and sighs,
Draped in a blanket of frost-kissed goodbyes.
"Do I really need to endure this each year?"
Whispers to snowflakes, some frozen in cheer.

Yet in dreams, it dances through sparkling frosts,
Imagining summers, and counting the costs.
For every leaf that fades with the chill,
A sense of renewal begins to fulfill.

In the Company of Foliage

In the corner sits a leafy friend,
Waving hello and refusing to bend.
“Oh, to be like you,” a plastic says bold,
“But do you even breathe? That's a sight to behold!”

With a quirk of its leaf, the plant gives a grin,
“Of course I do, just take it all in!”
The plastic rolls eyes, so stiff and so cold,
“Next thing you’ll say is you’re friends with the mold!”

They laugh together, it’s quite the odd pair,
One with stories, while the other stands there.
But who'd have thought there’d be such a vibe?
Plants make for pals—who needs a hive?

As sunlight pours in, the shadows do dance,
In their leafy world, there’s always a chance.
For friendships grow wildly, in their own funky way,
With giggles and sways, throughout the day.

The Lullaby of Watered Roots

When raindrops tap on the window’s pane,
A plant hums softly, “Come sing me again!”
With roots deep in love, it sways to the beat,
Sipping on droplets like a cherished treat.

“Oh, shower me more!” it shouts with glee,
“I’m the happiest plant you’ve ever seen,
With a wiggle and jiggle, and a bit of a twist,
Let me tell you now, I cannot resist!”

Friends across the room shake their heads in jest,
“Do plants actually dance? It’s a curious quest.”
But the truth is known to every leaf and sprout,
In the quiet of night, they sway about.

As morning comes up with a nod of the sun,
They laugh in chorus, “A new day’s begun!”
With droplets still whispering dreams in their roots,
The dance of the leaves is forever enroute.

Lament of the Houseplant

In a pot so wide and round,
I stretch my leaves, I stand my ground.
But dust bunnies think I’m their friend,
They settle in and refuse to bend.

Water me, oh human dear,
I promise I won’t disappear.
Yet you leave me here to dry,
While the cat gives me that sly eye.

With sunlight dancing on my face,
I long for a little more space.
Chlorophyll dreams in vibrant hues,
Yet I’m stuck in these silly shoes.

Oops! A leaf fell, what a mess!
Is this what you call plant stress?
If I could laugh, I’d share a joke,
But alas, I'm just a leafy bloke.

In the Stillness of Green

In a corner where light spills,
I sit and ponder, catching chills.
A spider leaves, what's the plan?
That crafty guy now thinks he's grand.

The neighbors whisper 'bout my glare,
They need to know I just don't care!
Growing slowly, gaining pride,
Why rush when you can take a ride?

My friends, the cacti, poke and tease,
"Come on, join us, won't you please?"
But their prickly games aren't for me,
I'm in a shade of mystery.

Yet here I stand, a leafy star,
Dreaming of adventures afar.
I just want to sip on sun,
But I might just stay, it's more fun.

Melancholy in the Garden

Amidst the blooms, I feel so blue,
With petals flair and colors too.
They giggle as I stretch so high,
And make me wonder, why oh why?

The daisies dance in killer heels,
While I'm stuck with my leafy feels.
They throw a party, flowers in bloom,
But I'm left here—left to fume!

"Hey plant friend, wanna join the fun?"
Oh sure, just me and my sad pun.
I could be the life of this place,
If only I had a little grace.

With leaves that sway in quiet hum,
I watch the petals strut their drum.
But one day soon, I'll join their crew,
With flashy fronds, a grand debut!

When Leaves Speak Softly

When dusk falls, and shadows play,
Our leaves conspire in a gentle sway.
“Did you hear what Fern just said?”
“Something funny ’bout a garden bed!”

We whisper tales of sunlit days,
Of rains that fell in perfect sprays.
Each droplet told a story true,
Of all the fun that we could pursue.

A bug stops by, thinks he’s so sly,
But let’s be real, he’s just a fly.
Our tales get tall, a riotous cheer,
Life in our green world brings us near.

So here we sit, in a leafy spree,
Sharing giggles, just us three.
In the stillness, we can conspire,
To dream of adventures that won’t tire!

Blues Beneath the Canopy

In a pot so small and round,
Leaves above look quite profound.
Sunlight hits, but water's shy,
One droop down, I hear it sigh.

Tangled roots in a race,
Chasing dreams of leafy space.
Throw a party, call the bees,
But tell them to mind their knees.

Plenty of jokes from the sun,
But photosynthesis? Not much fun!
Every day a new green hope,
But I'm just a plant, without a rope.

A leaf's dance, quite the jest,
Wobbling slowly, what a quest!
Grab your friends, it's time to sway,
With laughter growing every day.

When Leaves Weep in Silence

A droplet forms at leaf's end,
Is it rain, or just my friend?
Whispering tales of sunny days,
While I stand here in a haze.

Stretching wide, I wear my grin,
But deep within, where to begin?
Feeling jolly, not quite right,
Ticklish ground beneath moonlight.

Leafy friends snicker away,
'Join our club, come what may!'
I tap my foot, they laugh and spin,
Life of the party, can't let them win.

Oh, solace found in funny strife,
Leaves weep gently; that's the life.
Yet here I stand, no time to pout,
In this jungle, I'm never out.

Echoes of a Forgotten Plant

Dusty corners, where I lay,
Holding secrets, night and day.
In my pot, old stories sprout,
Whispers of laughter, twist about.

Once a star on window's ledge,
Now I'm stuck at nature's edge.
Rubbing elbows with the dust,
Trying hard, like leaves, I must.

A gnome's hat, a hedgehog's grin,
Where's the fun? Where do I begin?
Clouds drift past without a care,
While I ponder, spinning air.

Oh, echoes sing from soil below,
Nature's humor in this show.
Laughter grows amidst the gloom,
Planting joy, with room to bloom.

A Leaf's Lament

As the sun beams, I feel the glow,
But it's too hot; I'm moving slow.
Dancing shadows pass me by,
Hiding dreams as clouds roll high.

Pot-bound blues, a sad refrain,
With roots that yearn for endless rain.
Giggles echo, but here I stay,
Chasing shadows, day by day.

Once I swayed, so spry and free,
Now I joke, it's just me and me.
With each breeze, I'll spin and tilt,
In my world, where laughter's built.

Yet inside, there's always cheer,
Among the leaves, I'll persevere.
So let the world spin round and round,
In my heart, joy can be found.

Lessons from a Leaf

A leaf so wide, it steals the show,
Swaying in air, like it's on a row.
It spills its secrets, and oh, such lies,
Claiming the sun, while just feeling shy.

Tucked near the window, it bends with grace,
Sipping the rays, yet moving in place.
Whispers of wisdom from a verdant friend,
Lessons from leaves that never quite end.

Heartstrings and Houseplants

My plant's a diva, it strikes a pose,
With moody greens and flamboyant toes.
It sighs for water, yet thirsts for fame,
Demanding attention, it plays the game.

Each day, a drama, a leaf or two,
I swear it rolls eyes, or maybe it’s true.
Water a bit too much? It turns to pout,
Grow a little tall? It wants to shout!

Requiem for a Drying Leaf

Oh dear drying leaf, you've lost your flair,
Once vibrant and bold, now gasping for air.
Once you danced with joy in the morning light,
Now crumped and crisp, it’s quite the sight.

Rest gently, sweet leaf, your time has come,
As I laugh at your fate, how it’s all been so dumb.
But fear not, my friend, your memory will cling,
As I replace you with more vibrant bling.

The Colors of Loneliness

In a sea of green, one leaf feels blue,
Each sunbeam cast is the same old view.
As others turn lively, it shies from the fray,
Pondering shades that have gone astray.

Reflection in glass shows its wavering doubt,
"When will I thrive? Will I ever sprout?"
Yet laughter ensues, it's a comedic stance,
That even the saddest can still take a chance.

Tides of Dust and Desire

In the corner it stands, so green and so bold,
With dreams of a garden, yet it feels so old.
Dust gathers thick, like a thick winter coat,
It sighs in the silence, like a big, lazy goat.

Its leaves whisper tales of the days it once thrived,
Now counting the sun, feeling less than alive.
A watering can waits, it dreams of a pour,
While laughter erupts from its plant neighbor's lore.

Oh, leafy comrade, let's dance in the light,
We'll shake off our worries, it's a silly sight.
With rhythmic sways to the tunes of the breeze,
We'll chuckle and giggle, oh, whatever will please.

So here's to the plant with a heart full of wit,
For joy sprouts in laughter, and that's truly it.
As we bask in our glory, let's stay ever bright,
A quirky duo, thriving, in the soft twilight.

Serenade of the Sunlit Shade

In a sun-drenched window, the show must go on,
A leafy performer, from dusk until dawn.
With a bow made of sunlight, it takes center stage,
Flaunting each leaf like a dancer's new page.

The pot, it sings softly with a rhythmic beat,
While roots hold a secret, beneath dusty feet.
Giggles erupt from the soil below,
As the sunbeams applaud, putting on quite the show.

A pot full of laughter, a sprinkle of cheer,
It tickles the air as friends gather near.
Each leaf a story, each branch a new quirk,
Who knew such a plant could be quite the jerk?

So here in the shade, let's raise a good cheer,
To the riddles and romps that we hold most dear.
For in this small universe, where plants often croon,
We find joy in the dance and nature's sweet tune.

A Plant's Heartbeat

In the heart of the room, beats a leafy green pulse,
Tick tock goes the rhythm, a tangible impulse.
With each ray of sunlight, it wiggles a tad,
A plant's version of dance, though it looks quite mad.

It dreams of vast jungles, of wild, boundless space,
But mostly it lounges in its cozy place.
Beneath the faux sunlight it imagines a scene,
Where vines twist and twirl in a grand magazine.

With neighbors all creeping, it gives them a wink,
'Come, join in my fun!' as it starts to rethink.
In a pot that's too small, it wiggles and writhes,
A comedy show as it seeks to survive.

So cheers for the plant with its heart so alive,
Among kitchen utensils, it learns to thrive.
A heartbeat of humor in the simplest clime,
With each leaf a giggle, it weathered the time.

Whisper of Leaves in Twilight

As shadows grow longer, the leaves start to chat,
In whispers of twilight, just imagine that!
They swap tales of potting, and all that they've seen,
From battles with pests to the joys in between.

"Remember that time?" one leaf starts to croon,
When a rogue cat leaped and they were all strewn?
Laughter erupts in a soft, leafy chorus,
Echoing softly, like tales told before us.

The moon casts a glow, with silvery grace,
A gathering of greens in their favorite place.
With quirks and with tales, they revel and play,
As night wraps them up in a velvety sway.

So listen real close to your plants as they speak,
In whispers of wisdom, so quirky and sleek.
For in twilight's embrace, there's much to behold,
A world full of wonder, more precious than gold.

Solitude Amongst the Foliage

In my corner green, I sit in glee,
A jungle home, just my plant and me.
Conversations bloom, though one-sided thought,
A leaf says, ‘Hello!’ while I look distraught.

Chasing away the drab and the gray,
A palm’s dance moves brighten my day.
As vines crawl up the walls in delight,
I laugh at my pals, they just can’t get right.

The corner feels cozy, peace all around,
My leafy friends thrive, without making a sound.
With pots full of joy, I’m never alone,
In this leafy kingdom, I’ve made my throne.

Though they never judge when I spill the tea,
It’s hard being cool when they’re rooting for me.
Laughter and green, a quirky retreat,
Amongst these plants, I can't be beat!

Portrait of an Indoor Oasis

Welcome to my space, where green reigns supreme,
A rubber plant smiles, living the dream.
I gaze at the leaves, they can really sway,
As if they discuss my clumsiness today.

In light streaming in, the shadows engage,
My fern's quite the actor, stealing the stage.
Potted conversation, that's how we roll,
I pour them some water, they sip from the bowl.

A cactus rolls in, rather prickly and rude,
But the peace lily says, "Hey, let's keep it crude!"
Let's mingle it up with a humid dance,
Each leaf has a story, give yours a chance.

Together we laugh as the sun starts to set,
With foliage friends, I've no room for regret.
In this quirky portrait, there's humor to find,
Every leaf and each petal, a treasure so kind.

Dancing with Dust Motifs

In a world of green, I shimmy and sway,
With dust motes floating, they join in the play.
A quick little jig while I clean the shelf,
My plants cheer me on, 'You're your best self!'

They watch as I dust, a room full of life,
While pulling some strings, an indoor strife.
A spider plant giggles, 'You missed a spot!'
It's a raucous affair, and I've got a lot.

With my rubberized pals, there's a rhythm to keep,
Brushing aside cobwebs, I dive in the deep.
Twirling and laughing, the sunlight's just right,
At this gathering, I'm the star of the night.

When the chores meet the giggles, the atmosphere sings,
Together with dust, we've no cares or stings.
A dance of defeat, but I'm still feeling grand,
In my leafy abode, I make my own band!

Cascades of Urban Greenery

Living in concrete, a tropical spree,
My indoor jungle feels wild and free.
With pots on the windowsill, life's full of cheer,
Each leaf catches sunlight, a picnic, my dear.

As busyness buzzes, I hear the winds call,
Yet in my green haven, I rise and I fall.
A snake plant hisses, 'Keep calm in the heat!'
With friends made of chlorophyll, can't be beat!

Tiny rebels with roots dance through the grime,
They peek out the window, oh what a climb!
In this urban jungle, I've found my sweet spot,
Where laughter and foliage create quite a lot.

So here's to my plants, eclectic and grand,
They sway in the breeze, my nature's own band.
Living amidst concrete, I raise my glass high,
To cascades of greenery, I'm ready to fly!

A Symphony of Shadows

In my living room, greens take a stand,
With leaves like dancers, a jungle so grand.
They sway and they wave, but oh what a sight,
I wonder, do they party by day and by night?

In search of the sunlight, they stretch and they twist,
Each leaf has a story, can't let them be missed.
When guests come to dine, they steal the show,
A leafy brigade, putting on quite the glow!

They whisper sweet secrets, a botanical tune,
While I hold my breath under the watchful moon.
The shadows they cast, like puppets they play,
Oh, how I adore this green cabaret!

Yet when dust does gather, oh my, such a fuss,
They sulk like a kid when you don't share the bus.
I talk to them softly, beg, plead and coax,
For happiness dwells in these leafy folks.

Serenade for a Leafy Heart

Oh leafy companions, what tales you could tell,
Of sunny romance and times you fell.
You flirt with the sunlight, so bold and so grand,
While I sit in silence, a mug in my hand.

A leaf that once brilliant, now wilting in shame,
Accuses the pot for forgetting its name.
With soil so crammed, it could burst into tears,
We laugh through the sadness, embracing our fears.

When watering time strikes, a splash on the floor,
A dance of misfortune, oh what a chore!
The puddle's a stage, for ants that parade,
In a lively performance, a bug masquerade!

So here's to my plant pals, the chuckles we share,
In this leafy romance, we're quite the rare pair.
With laughter and leaves, life's never a bore,
In the garden of madness, who could ask for more?

Green Dreams and Gloom

My leafy prince sighs, oh the drama unfolds,
He's gone from bright green to a story retold.
I swear it's the light, it must have gone dim,
My once happy plant, now a sad, leafy whim.

With dreams of the jungle, he sang to the breeze,
But now there's a cloud, 'neath a frown from the trees.
"Water me gently!" he cries in despair,
While I keep my distance, hunting for air.

We joke about life, just a couple of greens,
In a world of neglect, it seems quite obscene.
With songs of mishap, our laughter rings clear,
In the chaos of potting, we've nothing to fear!

So here's to my leafy friend, what can we do?
Let's dance through this gloom, just me and you.
With water and sunshine, our spirits revive,
And together we'll thrive, oh, to be most alive!

Balancing Act of Nature

In pots they do balance, a leafy cabaret,
When it's time for a turn, they don't want to play.
One leans to the left, the other to right,
In a waltz of confusion, oh what a sight!

They clamored for sunshine, with ardor and cheer,
In pursuit of the light, they're bold pioneers.
But when I come near, with scissors in hand,
They act like they're injured, it's all quite unplanned.

Oh, nature's a circus, and I'm but the clown,
Trying not to drop them in a leafy breakdown.
One twist here, one trim there, oh what a dance,
With a snicker and snort, they sure take a chance!

Yet laughter remains, as we all find our roles,
In this balancing act, we're just planting souls.
So let's raise a toast, to the greens and the jokes,
In the theatre of nature, we're all just some folks!

Fragile Fortitude in Clay

In a pot of dreams I dwell,
My leaves shout, 'All is well!'
Yet one slight breeze does tease,
And down I flop, oh, dear trees!

Water me once, oh please,
Too much, and I'm in a squeeze.
Sunshine serenades my fate,
But shade's just a freckled mate.

I watch the world, what a show!
People passing to and fro.
Yet here I stand, a leafy clown,
With roots that never leave the town.

Oh, to dance on a summer’s day,
Yet fear the moment you splay.
Fragile heart in sturdy clay,
I giggle while I sway away.

A Soliloquy of Soil

Beneath the surface, funk and flair,
A worm’s life isn't done with care.
I wriggle and squirm in the muck,
Digging deep for my bit of luck.

Talk to me, oh mighty spade,
Your metal glistened, dreams displayed.
Invite the bugs, make a scene,
Together we form quite the routine!

My friends the roots offer advice,
'Just hang loose, don’t think twice!'
But there’s drama with every drop,
When raindrops fall, I hop and plop.

Spinning tales in earthy loam,
With every twist, I call it home.
A little humor keeps me spry,
In soil's grasp, I reach for the sky.

Breathing in Botanical Blues

My leaves are waving, what's the fuss?
A voice from the pot—a little plus!
Swaying side to side, I croon,
'Hang tight, spring will come soon!'

Breath of life, a chlorophyll spree,
But please don’t brush against me!
I’ll twitch and shake, a botanic dance,
Yet one too many bumps, my chance!

With roots that tangle in delight,
I giggle softly through the night.
Under moonlight, oh, the sights!
I laugh at clouds, oh, what a flight!

In shades of green, I spin my yarn,
With a wink and wave—a leafy charm.
Breathing in laughs, a joyous muse,
Adventures of a plant, sans the blues.

Pensive Moments in Verdancy

Sitting here on a sunny perch,
In leafy thoughts, I softly lurch.
'What's that? A drip! My leaves want more!'
I guess hydration's my one true chore.

Wobbling with wisdom, I muse all day,
About soil and sun—my verdant ballet.
In each quiet breath, what do I see?
A world of humans busy, not like me!

I tap my roots to a beat so fine,
Creating a rhythm in nature's design.
With cautious giggles, I sway and lean,
In my plantly thoughts, I'm a serene queen.

Moments pensive, yet filled with cheer,
As I watch the seasons pass, year by year.
In verdant dreams, I giggle and dwell,
Among thoughts of soil, I'm under a spell.

The Aches of Indoor Growing

I watered you last week, oh dear,
But you still look quite severe.
Your leaves are droopy, what a sight,
Did you rebel against the light?

A sunbeam's warmth, you do ignore,
While I run laps across the floor.
With every droplet I now pour,
You stare at me—what more's in store?

I can't grip on to my green dream,
Your stubbornness makes me want to scream!
The plant doctor says your roots are tight,
Yet here I stand, just full of fright!

So here we are, both caught in this dance,
You sulk in dirt while I take a chance.
Each day we battle, you and me,
Indoor gardening is not for the faint of heart, you see!

Gloom Beneath the Foliage

In shadows deep, your leaves reside,
Oh, what a gloomy little ride!
I hang on tight, it's hard to smile,
Your pouty vibe makes it worth my while.

A droplet falls, you drop it too,
You sulk as if you really knew.
Photosynthesis is just a joke,
With every breath, I pass and choke.

You flaunt your leaves like drama queens,
While I sip tea and plot my schemes.
Oh, what escapades we could unveil,
If only you would follow the trail!

But leaf by leaf, and sigh by sigh,
We bumble along, you and I.
In this indoor tale of gloom and mirth,
Just know, dear plant, you're well worth my worth!

Green Melodies in a Dusty Corner

Dusty corner, what a stage!
Your leaves like music, full of gauge.
Yet here I sit with scrub and broom,
As you bask in that corner gloom.

Oh, how I sing for you each noon,
A lopsided tune, a little croon.
But those bugs creep in, oh my!
They waltz with pride, while I just sigh.

A little sun would cure your woes,
Yet you cling to your rooty throes.
You sway and sway, a funny jig,
While I just watch—oh, how you dig!

So here's my song of leafy cheer,
We'll dance in circles, year by year.
From a dusty chair, I still believe,
In our green melodies, I won't leave!

Jangled Roots and Fading Leaves

Oh tangled roots, a jangle mess,
You stretch and pout, I must confess.
Your leaves are fading, once so bright,
Now they grumble in the dim light.

I'll serenade you with my woes,
As you play hard to catch, who knows?
A shuffle here, a twist or two,
And yet you sit like you're taboo!

Jangled roots, let's have a plan,
You're not a diva, nor a grandstand!
Just an indoor friend, live and free,
Let's groove together in harmony!

But still, I squint at your despair,
Are you just giving me the stare?
In this game, I'm not a fool,
Let's get those roots to play it cool!

Shadows Dance on Leafy Shoulders

In the corner where sunlight beams,
They sway and twist, like living dreams.
With laughter, they wiggle, no care in sight,
Their leafy dance brings pure delight.

Oh, how they prance, with stems so tall,
Pretending to be the stars at a ball.
A party of greens, inviting the sun,
They chuckle softly, a leafy pun.

Fronds like friends, a whimsical crew,
High-fiving shadows, spreading the hue.
Each wiggle and jiggle, a sight to behold,
In the dance of the leaves, stories unfold.

The catwalk of greens, strutting with flair,
On the edge of the sill, without a care.
Betwixt sunbeams, they curl and tease,
In a world made of laughter, they aim to please.

The Invisible Weight of Growth

Oh, the pressure of growing, it’s quite absurd,
Like a tree with no roots, just absurd!
Stretching for sunlight, it’s a daily craze,
With delicate leaves in an existential phase.

Tugging and pulling, they hope not to break,
While plotting their next snack, for their growth's sake.
“Do I need more water, or just a friend?”
The whispering foliage has no clear end.

Each inch is a triumph, each leaf brings a smile,
While secretly wishing for a rest for a while.
The pressure’s immense, yet they stand so proud,
A botanical sitcom, drawing a crowd.

Underneath it all, they giggle and stretch,
Playing the game of growth—what a sketch!
As the world rushes by, they remain aloof,
Waving at worries from their leafy roof.

Symphony of a Silent Sill

On the windowsill, a concert begins,
With leaves as the stars, and sunlight as spins.
A rustling crescendo, a giggle or two,
As the breeze slips through, they hum something new.

Chlorophyll notes dance across the air,
Each rustle a joke, light as a prayer.
They chatter in whispers, oh what a glee!
Creating a rumble, just for me.

Silent, yes, but not without flair,
These green little wonders, a musical pair.
With every fresh wave from the soft summer breath,
The sound of their laughter defies even death.

From the harmony bright, a melody grows,
In the symphony of greens, weariness goes.
So here's to the sill, where they quietly play,
With a song in each leaf, and sunshine to sway.

Longing Within the Leafy Borders

Beyond the window, adventures do call,
But here in the pot, they're stuck at the hall.
Leaning and yearning, their roots read the map,
While dreaming of journeys, wrapped up in a gap.

While wishing for breezes, they ponder the skies,
'Can we reach out, or are we too shy?'
The dust on the sill seems to giggle and tease,
As they ponder their fate with a hint of unease.

The world outside calls with a vibrant allure,
Yet here they stand, feeling so unsure.
'What if we fall? Oh, what if we fly?'
In leafy debates, loud hopes start to sigh.

They dream of the jungle, the wild, and the free,
While stuck in the pot, with just dreams to see.
But the whispers of green hold a promise so bright,
"Adventure awaits, just beyond the light!"

Impressions on Pottery

A pot full of dreams, small and wide,
Hoping for rain, though dry inside.
Each leaf a whisper, each stem a dance,
I talk to my plant, it never takes a chance.

Around it, I juggle my thoughts and glares,
Who knew that leaves could spark such cares?
I swear it winks, oh what a trick!
Is this my plant or a green magic stick?

It grows with a flair, it sways with a grin,
While I'm stuck guessing just where to begin.
So here I am, a gardener lost,
Crafting pot jokes, but at what cost?

In the sun's warm light, they beg for a cheer,
Foliage fashion, is that what's here?
I prune with a laugh, in joy and dismay,
Who knew clay and green could brighten my day?

The Weight of Undying Leaves

Oh, those endless greens, they shine so bright,
Yet here in my room, they start a fight.
A leaf took a dive, and what a scene!
It stalks my floor, like a rogue beanstalk keen.

With laughter I tease, as I clean each mess,
This plant's my joy, though a source of stress.
It leans on my chair; I say "not today!"
But it still stands proud, in its leafy ballet.

A weight on my heart, more than soil or sun,
Each leaf holds a quirk—it's all in good fun.
I swear it starts chuckling, a green leafy jest,
Making me ponder which one is the best.

In the corner it giggles with glee like a child,
Each strip of green mischief, oh so wild.
Left a bit lonely, but never quite blue,
This plant's a page-turner, my own leafy view.

Refrains of the Repotted

In a new pot it sighs, as if to complain,
A fresh batch of dirt brings accolades and pain.
It settles in snug, a diva on stage,
Pouting for water, oh what a rampage!

"Oh, darling!" I laugh as it wobbles and sways,
Don't you know life's an infinite maze?
With every new home, there's growth and delight,
Yet here you act like a star in the night!

Tell me, dear friend, is that leaf a bit smirked?
On days like these, my sanity's worked.
You're shouting for sun while your roots demand cheer—

I'm just a mere human, oh please, lend an ear!

From pot to pot, oh what a spree,
Each root insists on another TV.
Yet here we are, you and I, in good cheer,
A bond over laughter, let's make that clear.

Lost in Leafy Elegance

A tall green friend, so bold and grand,
Sways in the wind, understands my plan.
With every twist, each turn, what fun!
It laughs at the sun as it chases a run.

"Oh to be leaves!" I wish I could say,
"Elegance found in bright, leafy play!"
Yet here on the ground, I plod and I toil,
While my plant raises brows in the rich, dark soil.

Attend to my friend, it demands with flair,
A sprinkle of water, some love, and some care.
Oh perfect companion, with humor so sleek,
Your fancy demeanor makes me feel meek.

Yet here I remain, oh what bitter tease!
A life bound by rules while your curves dance with ease.
So here's to the leaves that giggle and sway,
Lost in their elegance, come what may!

Mourning for the Sun

Oh, bright star in the sky, where do you go?
Your warmth is my dance, my leafy limbo.
When clouds roll by, I feel so sad,
Without your glow, I can't be glad.

I stretch my arms, I reach so wide,
In shadows I hide, it's hard to abide.
My neighbors all laugh; they shine so fair,
But I'm the one stuck with leaf underwear!

I sigh to the moon, such silly blooms,
Wishing for sunlight in dreary rooms.
A little sunbeam, that's all I need,
To dance like the others, to finally succeed!

So here's to the sun, my favorite tease,
I'll tickle the roots and dance in the breeze.
With every week that passes by,
I promise to grow - oh me, oh my!

Leafy Confessions

In the corner of the room, I stand so proud,
With leaves all green, like a velvet crowd.
But come on, I confess, I'm quite the flop,
I bend in the breeze, and I just can't stop!

My friends all whisper, they snicker and jest,
"Look at that plant, at its leafy quest!"
I wriggle and wiggle, a leafy ballet,
But every mishap just steals my display!

I tried to grow tall, thought I'd reach for the sky,
Instead, I'm just a shrub with a curious eye.
I dream of the jungle, wild and free,
But instead, I'm here, sipping tea with the bee!

So here's to my awkward, ungraceful sprawl,
I may be a jokester, but I stand tall.
With each silly twist, I've found my own groove,
In this leafy life, I've learned how to move!

An Ode to the Unbending

Oh mighty plant, so stiff and spry,
You stand there proud, reaching for the sky.
Your neighbors all sway with the wind's gentle hand,
But you hold your ground, like a rock in the sand.

"To bend or not to bend," that is your creed,
While I'm over here, struggling to succeed.
I envy your strength as I quiver and shake,
You mock me, dear friend, for goodness' sake!

With every storm that rumbles and roars,
You hold fast, while I'm stuck at the doors.
You laugh at the gusts and the playful breeze,
While I'm folding up, begging for ease.

So here's to the unbending, oh how I cheer!
While I twist and shout, you'll still be right here.
With roots deep in laughter and leaves to the sun,
You're my leafy hero, the proud and the fun!

Cradled by Nature's Grace

In the glow of the morning, I wake with a stretch,
My leaves all a-quiver, it's nature's sketch.
Each droplet of dew, like a sweet little kiss,
Promising laughter, how could I miss?

The sunlight tickles, a warm, playful tease,
I sway with the music, like a leaf in the breeze.
With roots deep in soil and dreams up above,
I dance in the light, oh what could I love?

My friends all chime in, a botanical choir,
We hum to the rhythm, our leafy attire.
With every giggle, a blossom appears,
In this silly garden, there's nothing but cheers!

So cradled by nature, I laugh and I sway,
With leaves dancing freely, I'm here to stay.
Among all the blooms, I'll shout and I'll sing,
In this whimsical world, I'm the queen of the fling!

Resilience in the Rain

Raindrops dance on leaves, oh so cheeky,
Bouncing off blooms, feeling quite freaky.
A splash here, a splash there, making a scene,
Nature's comedy in shades of green.

Bend, don’t break, that’s the game we play,
Giggling at storms, come what may.
Dancing like it’s a lush, leafy ball,
With no care at all, just embracing the squall.

So here we stand, vibrant and spry,
Letting the rain take us high in the sky.
Our roots digging deep, while we sway and spin,
In the rhythm of life, it's a win-win-win!

So come join the party, don’t sit on the fence,
In the rain, we’ll find joy, it’s truly intense.
With laughter and joy, and wiggles all around,
In the heart of the chaos, pure happiness found.

Enchanted by Green Whispers

A leaf whispered secrets, soft and low,
Of sunlight adventures, that made it glow.
A dance with the breeze, oh what a delight,
The silly antics of plants take flight.

Fluttering petals, like butterflies tease,
Spinning their tales with the greatest of ease.
Gossiping roots twist beneath the earth,
Sharing their stories, revealing their worth.

Leaves cracking jokes in the vibrant sun,
Swaying and laughing, oh aren’t we fun?
Who knew greenery could have such a laugh,
Each moment a pleasure, each sunbeam a gaffe!

In the shade of a tree, we gather and cheer,
Nature's comedy club, our laughter sincere.
With every green whisper, another giggle grows,
A nature-made marvel, full of silly shows.

Rippling Through the Canopy

Through the leaves, a breeze does tickle,
Whispers and giggles, it starts to wiggle.
Up above, the branches lean and sway,
Creating a canopy, a colorful play.

Each ripple a chuckle, each sway a grin,
As shadows parade, letting the fun begin.
The dance of the trees, a delightful routine,
A hilarious waltz, if you know what I mean.

The sunbeams peek through in a game of hide,
As foliage shimmies, oh what a ride!
Greenery giggles, what a sight to behold,
With every rustle, new stories unfold.

In the map of the leaves, adventures unwind,
Laughing at life, with nature aligned.
In the warmth of the canopy, we find our tune,
As laughter floats up, like a bright summer noon.

The Weight of Quiet Growth

In the silence, we grow, nearly stealthy,
Unseen yet thriving, feeling quite wealthy.
With roots like a party, underground they cheer,
While the world above remains unaware, dear.

Creeping up slowly, with grace in each inch,
Petals and leaves in a mischievous pinch.
Who’s to say silence is not full of fun?
When the hidden dance is just about to run!

Tension in the air, as we stretch for the light,
Chasing the sun, with a grin, oh so bright.
In this quiet game, laughter’s the key,
For who knows the joy of a slow, giddy spree?

So while we grow steady, in laughter we bond,
Plant friends together, of whom we're so fond.
In the weight of our patience, there's much to find,
A funny little tale, for the gentle and kind.

www.ingramcontent.com/pod-product-compliance
Lightning Source LLC
Chambersburg PA
CBHW072223070526
44585CB00015B/1469